Paracord Crafts

LEISURE ARTS, INC.
Maumelle, Arkansas

THINGS YOU NEED TO KNOW

*To make your crafting fun and easy, please read **Things You Need To Know** (pages 2-3) and **How To Trim And Singe** (page 24) before beginning your project.*

Paracord, aka parachute cord, is a super-strong nylon cord that comes in lots of colors and patterns.

For a military person or outdoor enthusiast, a length of paracord makes a handy survival tool which can be used as a clothesline, replace a broken shoelace, hold up a makeshift tent, and much more. A long piece of paracord can be tied into a series of knots that reduces the length making it easier to pack or carry. The knots can be untied to use the cord as needed.

For the rest of us, paracord makes a real fashion statement when tied into knotted accessories like bracelets and key fobs. It can even jazz up flip flops or headbands! The projects in this book are quick and easy to make, cool to use, and a great way to keep some paracord with you all the time—because you just never know when you might need a bit of cord.

WHAT KIND OF PARACORD TO USE

All the projects in this book are made with #550 paracord. It is easy to find in craft/hobby, discount, and military surplus stores and comes in different size hanks. The instructions in this book are based on 16' hanks, but you may not use the whole hank for a project.

When cut lengths are given in the project instructions, the lengths always includes a little extra cord—it's better to have too much than to run short. When no cut lengths are given, you will need the entire 16' length.

SAFETY IS IMPORTANT

CAUTION: These projects involve the use of sharp objects and open flames. Adult supervision is required at all times.

OTHER SUPPLIES YOU WILL NEED

One of the great things about paracord crafting is you don't need a lot of supplies. With just some cord, utility scissors, a multi-purpose lighter, and a ruler, tape measure, or yardstick, you can make a Loop and Knot Bracelet. Add a ½" or ⅝" wide side-release buckle to make a Buckle Bracelet. Some tape (masking, painter's, or duct) is useful for securing cords while you knot.

HOW TO SIZE A BRACELET

Measure your wrist and decide how loose or tight you want your bracelet. This measurement is your finished bracelet size.

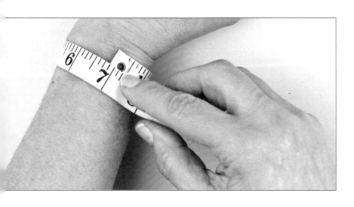

Working cord(s) or working end(s) refers to the cord(s) or cord end(s) in use.

Standing cord(s) refers to the cord(s) not being used to tie or that are secured to your work surface.

"Right cord" or "left cord" refers to the position of the cords as they face you when you are knotting unless otherwise noted in your project instructions.

CHAIN SINNET BRACELETS

SHOPPING LIST

- ☐ 550 paracord (one 16' hank will make 2 bracelets)
- ☐ 2 large-hole beads (optional)
- ☐ utility scissors
- ☐ tape measure, ruler, or yardstick
- ☐ multi-purpose lighter

Note: This bracelet does not open and close with a loop and knot or a buckle so it needs to be loose enough to slip on and off your hand.

STEP 1 Cut one 8' length of paracord.

STEP 2 Make a loop in the center of the paracord. Wrap the right working cord around the loop and bring the working end under the wrap. Pull the cords to make a loose knot; do not over-tighten. The left cord will become the sliding cord. *(Figs. 1-2)*.

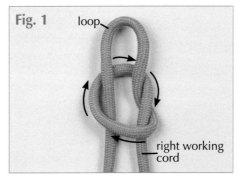

Fig. 1

loop

right working cord

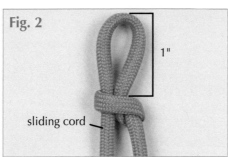

Fig. 2

1"

sliding cord

STEP 3 Turn the cords so that the sliding cord is on the right. Insert the folded left cord through the sliding cord loop *(Fig. 3)*.

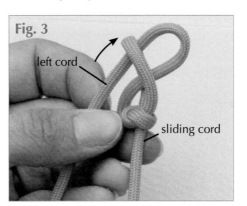

Fig. 3

left cord

sliding cord

STEP 4 Pull the sliding cord to tighten *(Fig. 4)*.

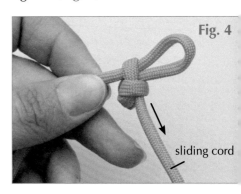

Fig. 4

sliding cord

STEP 5 The cord on the left now becomes the sliding cord. Insert the folded right cord into the sliding cord loop and tighten *(Figs. 5-6)*.

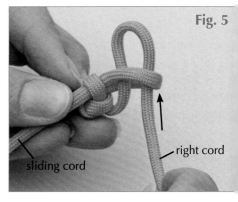

Fig. 5

sliding cord

right cord

Fig. 6

STEP 6 Continue making loops, alternating left and right cords until the bracelet is the right size *(Fig. 7)*.

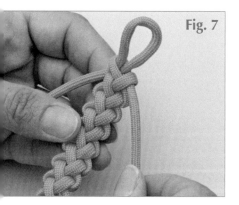
Fig. 7

STEP 7 To close the bracelet, tug on the first knot made to open the first loop *(Fig. 8)*. Insert the last loop made into the opened loop *(Figs. 9-10)*.

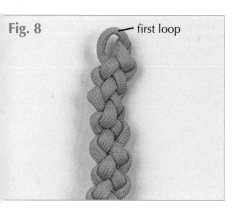
Fig. 8 — first loop

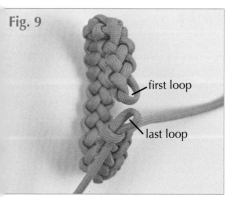
Fig. 9

first loop

last loop

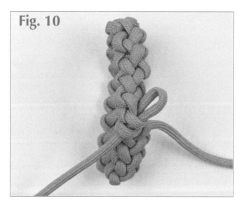
Fig. 10

STEP 8 Insert the non-sliding cord through the loop. Pull on both cord ends to tighten the knot *(Fig. 11)*.

Fig. 11

STEP 9 If desired, add a bead to each cord end. **Trim and Singe** (page 24) the ends.

STITCHED SOLOMAN BAR BRACELETS

SHOPPING LIST

- ☐ 550 paracord (one 16' hank for a one color bracelet **or** one 16' hank of **each** color for a two color bracelet)
- ☐ ½" wide side-release buckle (for a one color bracelet)
- ☐ utility scissors
- ☐ tape measure, ruler, or yardstick
- ☐ multi-purpose lighter
- ☐ masking, painter's, or duct tape (optional)

Tip: Taping down the top loop or buckle and the standing cord ends or bottom buckle makes it easier to tie knots around the standing cords.

LOOP AND KNOT BRACELET

STEP 1 Cut one 11' length of paracord for the working cords and one 5' length of paracord for the standing cords.

STEP 2 Fold the standing cord in half and center it on the working cord *(Fig. 1)*.

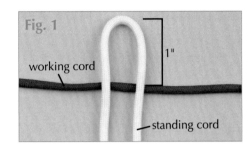

Fig. 1

working cord

1"

standing cord

STEP 3 Bring the right working cord over the standing cords. Bring the left working cord over and around the right working cord, behind the standing cords, and through the loop on the right side *(Fig. 2)*; pull the cords to tighten.

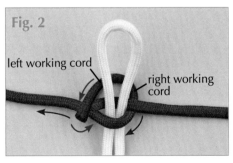

Fig. 2

left working cord

right working cord

STEP 4 Bring the left working cord between the standing cords and the right working cord behind the standing cords. Bring the working cord ends through the side loops *(Fig. 3)*; tighten.

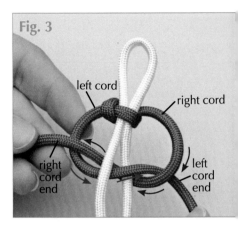

Fig. 3

left cord

right cord

right cord end

left cord end

STEP 5 Bring the right working cord between the standing cords and the left working cord behind the standing cords. Bring the working cord ends through the side loops *(Fig. 4)*; tighten.

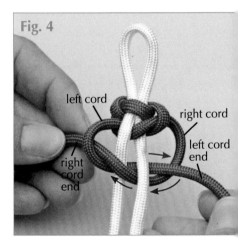

Fig. 4

left cord

right cord

right cord end

left cord end

STEP 6 Repeat Steps 4-5 *(Fig. 5)*, stopping when the knotted section is 1" short of your finished bracelet size.

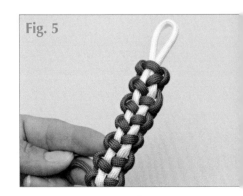

Fig. 5

STEP 2 Thread the cord ends through the remaining buckle piece from front to back and position the buckle at your finished bracelet size *(Fig. 9)*.

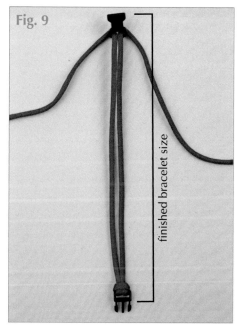

Fig. 9

finished bracelet size

STEP 7 On the wrong side, thread the working cord ends under the last knot *(Fig. 6)*; tighten. **Trim and Singe** (page 24) the ends.

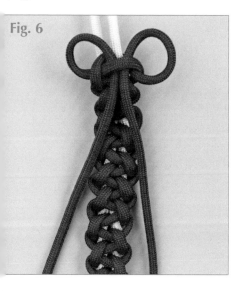

Fig. 6

STEP 8 Use the standing cords to make a **Diamond Knot** (page 23).

BUCKLE BRACELET

STEP 1 Fold the cord in half and insert the loop through one buckle piece from front to back. Bring the cords through the loop *(Fig. 7)*; pull to tighten *(Fig. 8)*.

Fig. 7

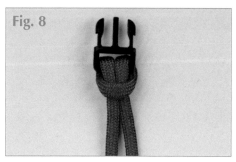

Fig. 8

STEP 3 Bring the left working cord over the standing cords and behind the right working cord. Bring the right working cord behind the standing cords and over the left working cord *(Fig. 10)*; tighten.

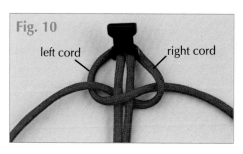

Fig. 10

left cord   right cord

STEP 4 Repeat Steps 4-5 of **Loop And Knot Bracelet**, until you reach the beginning buckle.

STEP 5 Referring to *Fig. 6*, thread the working cord ends under the last knot; tighten. **Trim and Singe** (page 24) the ends.

COBRA STITCH BRACELETS

SHOPPING LIST

- ☐ 550 paracord (one 16' hank for a one color bracelet **or** one 16' hank of **each** color for a two color bracelet)
- ☐ ½" wide side-release buckle (optional)
- ☐ utility scissors
- ☐ tape measure, ruler, or yardstick
- ☐ multi-purpose lighter
- ☐ masking, painter's, or duct tape (optional)

Tip: *Taping down the top loop or buckle and the standing cord ends or bottom buckle makes it easier to tie knots around the standing cords.*

ONE COLOR BRACELET WITH A LOOP AND KNOT

STEP 1 Cut one 11' length of paracord for the working cords and and one 5' length of paracord for the standing cords.

STEP 2 Fold the standing cord in half and center it on the working cord *(Fig. 1)*.

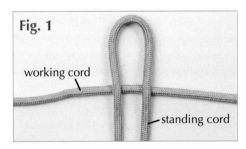

Fig. 1

working cord

standing cord

STEP 3 Bring the right working cord over the standing cords and behind the left working cord. Bring the right working cord through the loop created on the right side *(Fig. 2)*; pull the cords to tighten.

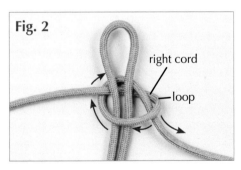

Fig. 2

right cord

loop

STEP 4 Bring the right working cord over the standing cords and behind the left working cord. Bring the left working cord behind the standing cords and over the right working cord *(Fig. 3)*; tighten.

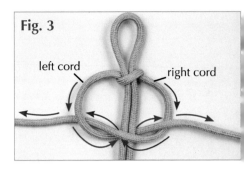

Fig. 3

left cord

right cord

STEP 5 Bring the left working cord over the standing cords and behind the right working cord. Bring the right working cord behind the standing cords and over the left working cord *(Fig. 4)*; tighten.

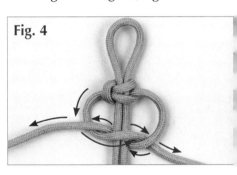

Fig. 4

STEP 6 Repeat Steps 4-5, stopping when the knotted section is 1" short of your finished bracelet size.

STEP 7 On the wrong side, thread the working cords under the last 2 knots *(Fig. 5)*; tighten. **Trim and Singe** (page 24) the ends.

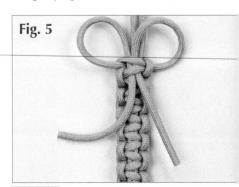

Fig. 5

STEP 8 Use the standing cords to make a **Diamond Knot** (page 23).

TWO COLOR BRACELET WITH A LOOP AND KNOT

CAUTION: Always keep your fingers away from the flame and never touch a melted cord end until it has cooled completely.

STEP 1 Cut a 6' length of **each** paracord color for the working cords. Cut a 5' length of one paracord color for the standing cords.

STEP 2 To join the two 6' cords into a single cord, hold both cords in one hand and **Singe** (page 24) the ends *(Fig. 6)*. *Quickly* press the hot ends together and hold until cool and the ends are fused together *(Figs. 7-8)*.

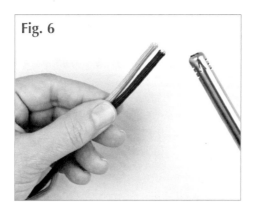

Fig. 6

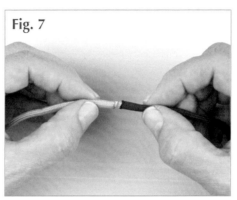

Fig. 7

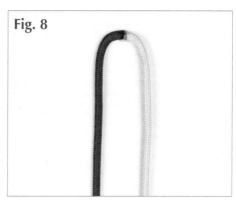

Fig. 8

STEP 3 Follow Steps 2-8 of **One Color Bracelet With A Loop And Knot** to knot and finish your bracelet.

Tip: This technique takes a little practice and might be easier if one person handles the cords and another applies the heat.

Continued on page 10.

Cobra Stitch Bracelets continued.

ONE COLOR BRACELET WITH BUCKLE
(shown on page 9)

STEP 1 Fold the cord in half and insert the loop through one buckle piece from front to back. Bring the cords through the loop *(Fig. 9)*; pull the cords to tighten.

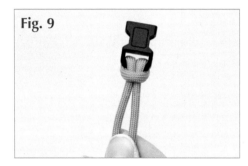

Fig. 9

STEP 2 Thread the cord ends through the remaining buckle piece and position the buckle at your finished bracelet size *(Fig. 10)*.

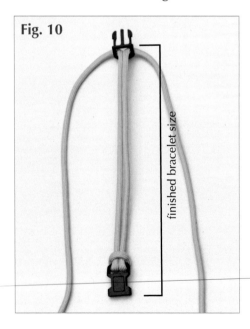

Fig. 10

finished bracelet size

STEP 3 Follow Steps 4-5 of **One Color Bracelet With A Loop And Knot** (page 8) to tie a series of **Cobra Stitch** knots *(Fig. 11)*, ending at the beginning buckle.

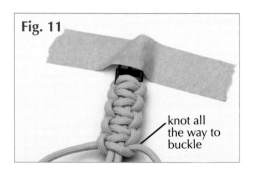

Fig. 11

knot all the way to buckle

STEP 4 On the wrong side, thread the working cord ends under the last knot *(Fig. 12)*; tighten. **Trim and Singe** (page 24) the ends.

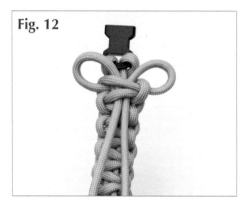

Fig. 12

TWO COLOR BRACELET WITH A BUCKLE
(shown on page 9)

STEP 1 Cut a 12' length of *each* paracord color.

STEP 2 Insert about 2" of each cord through one end of the buckle. **Singe** (page 24), then quickly press the hot cord ends to the corresponding cords *(Fig. 13)*.

Tip: An alternative to fusing is to secure the ends to the cord with a narrow piece of tape (Fig. 14).

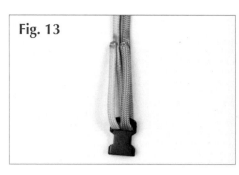

Fig. 13

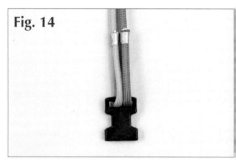

Fig. 14

STEP 3 Thread the cord ends through the remaining buckle piece and position the buckle at your finished bracelet size *(Fig. 15)*.

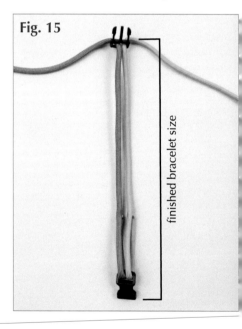

Fig. 15

finished bracelet size

STEP 4 Follow Steps 4-5 of **One Color Bracelet With A Loop And Knot** (page 8) to tie a series of **Cobra Stitch** knots, ending at the beginning buckle.

STEP 5 Follow Step 4 of **One Color Bracelet With A Buckle** to finish your bracelet.

YOU CAN ALSO MAKE

To add some bling to your bracelet, follow **One Color Bracelet With A Buckle** (left) and slide beads onto the standing cords between **Cobra Stitch** knots as desired.

For the headband, refer to page 9, Step 2, to fuse two 6' cords together. Starting on one end, tie **Cobra Stitch** knots around the headband. When you get to the other end, refer to page 10, *Fig. 12*, to finish the cord ends.

To jazz up your flops, refer to page 13, *Fig. 10*, to attach two 16' cord lengths to the center of one flip flop with a looped knot. Use one cord of each color to tie **Cobra Stitch** knots along each strap. When you get to the end of the strap, refer to page 10, *Fig. 12*, to finish the cord ends.

RAISING THE BAR BRACELETS

Tip: Taping down the top loop or buckle and the standing cord ends or bottom buckle makes it easier to tie knots around the standing cords.

LOOP AND KNOT BRACELET

STEP 1 Fold one cord in half and center it on the second cord. Bring the right cord over the standing and left working cord. Bring the right working cord through the loop created on the right side *(Fig. 1)*. Pull the cords to tighten.

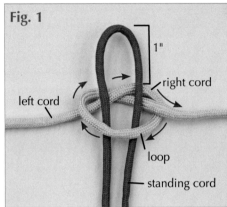

Fig. 1

1"
right cord
left cord
loop
standing cord

STEP 2 Turn cords over so the knot is on the top. Using one cord of each color as the working cords, wrap the right and then the left working cords around the standing cords *(Fig. 2)*; tighten *(Fig. 3)*.

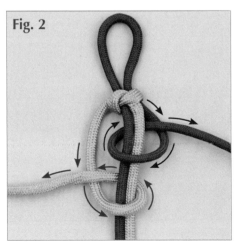

Fig. 2

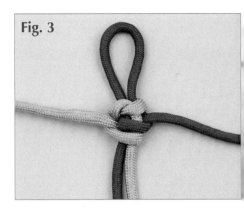

Fig. 3

STEP 3 Alternating right and left cords, repeat Step 2 until the knotted section is 1" short of your finished bracelet size *(Figs. 4-5)*.

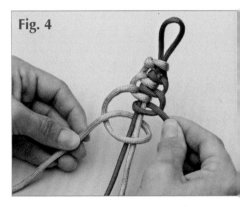

Fig. 4

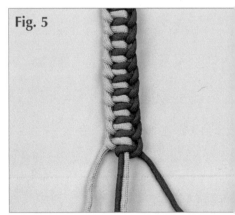

Fig. 5

STEP 4 On the wrong side, thread the working cords under the last knot *(Fig. 6)*; tighten. **Trim and Singe** (page 24) the ends *(Fig. 7)*.

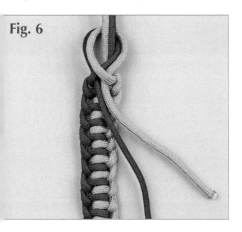
Fig. 6

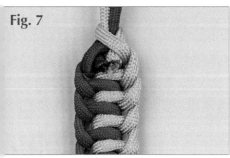
Fig. 7

STEP 5 Use the standing cords to make a **Diamond Knot** (page 23).

BUCKLE BRACELET

STEP 1 Fold both cords in half and insert one cord through each buckle opening from front to back *(Fig. 8)*.

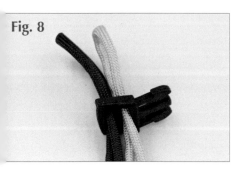
Fig. 8

STEP 2 Bring all four cord ends through both loops *(Fig. 9)*; pull the cords to tighten *(Fig. 10)*.

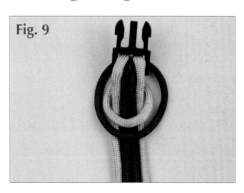
Fig. 9

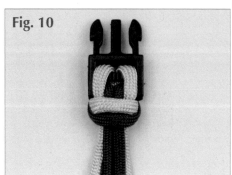
Fig. 10

STEP 3 Follow Steps 2-3 of **Loop And Knot Bracelet** to tie a series of **Raising The Bar** knots, stopping 1" short of your finished bracelet size.

STEP 4 Thread all four cord ends through the remaining buckle piece from front to back.

STEP 5 On the wrong side, thread the standing cord ends under the last knot; **Trim and Singe** (page 24) the cord ends. Repeat, to secure the working cord ends under the next-to-last knot *(Fig. 11)*.

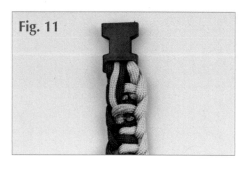
Fig. 11

TRILOBITE BRACELETS

SHOPPING LIST

- ☐ 550 paracord (one 16' hank of **each** color for a two color loop and knot bracelet) **or** one 16' hank for a one color buckle bracelet
- ☐ ⅝" wide side-release buckle (optional)
- ☐ utility scissors
- ☐ tape measure, ruler, or yardstick
- ☐ multi-purpose lighter
- ☐ masking, painter's, or duct tape

Tip: Taping down the top loop or buckle and the standing cord ends or bottom buckle makes it easier to tie knots around the standing cords.

LOOP AND KNOT BRACELET

STEP 1   Holding one cord of each color together, fold the cords in half and tape the center loop to your work surface.

STEP 2   *Note: You will be working towards the beginning loop.* Using 1 working cord of each color, begin knotting at your finished bracelet size minus 1" *(Fig. 1)*.

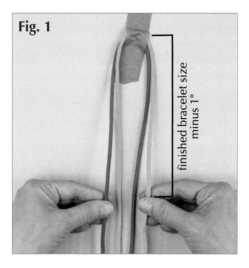

Fig. 1

finished bracelet size minus 1"

STEP 3   Bring the right working cord over the standing cords and under the left working cord *(Fig. 2)*.

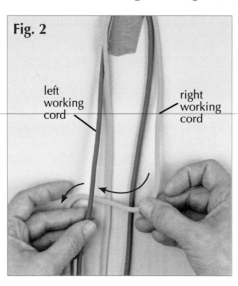

Fig. 2

left working cord

right working cord

STEP 4   Bring left working cord under the standing cords and over the right outer standing cord *(Fig. 3)*; pull the working cords to tighten.

Tip: The cord passing from right to left always crosses over the standing cords and the one passing from left to right always crosses under the standing cords.

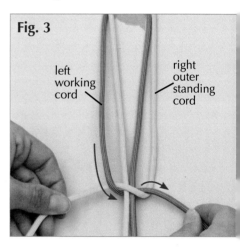

Fig. 3

left working cord

right outer standing cord

STEP 5   Bring the right working cord under the right outer cord, over the standing cords, and under the left outer cord; do not tighten *(Fig. 4)*.

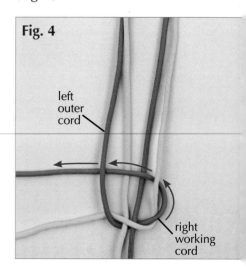

Fig. 4

left outer cord

right working cord

STEP 6 Bring left working cord over the left outer cord, under the standing cords and over the right outer cord *(Fig. 5)*; pull the working cords to tighten.

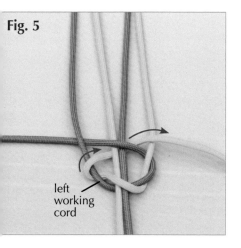

Fig. 5

left working cord

STEP 7 Repeat Steps 5-6 *(Figs. 6-7)* until the knotted section is 1" short of the beginning loop.

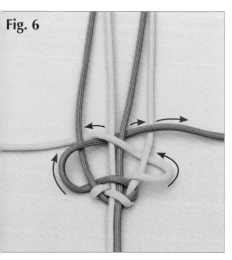

Fig. 6

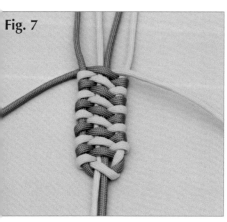

Fig. 7

STEP 8 On the wrong side, thread the working cords under the last 2 knots (page 10, *Fig. 12*); **Trim and Singe** (page 24) the ends.

STEP 9 Use the standing cords to make a **Diamond Knot** (page 23).

BUCKLE BRACELET

STEP 1 Cut one 13' and one 3' length of paracord.

STEP 2 Fold both cords in half and insert the 3' cord through the lower buckle opening and the 13' cord through the upper buckle opening from front to back *(Figs. 8-9)*.

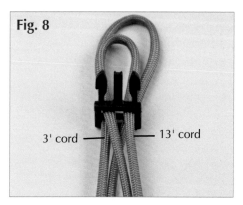

Fig. 8

3' cord — — 13' cord

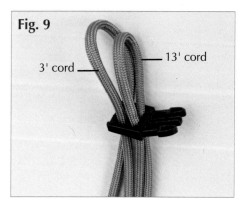

Fig. 9

3' cord — — 13' cord

Continued on page 16.

Trilobite Buckle Bracelet continued.

STEP 3 Bring all four cord ends through both loops *(Fig. 10)*; pull cords to tighten *(Fig. 11)*.

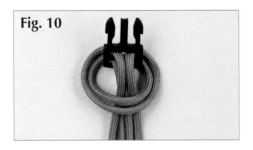

Fig. 10

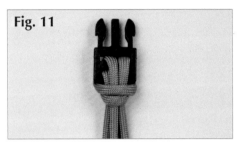

Fig. 11

STEP 4 Keeping the shorter cords in the center, thread all 4 cord ends through the other buckle piece from front to back and position the buckle at your finished bracelet size *(Fig. 12)*.

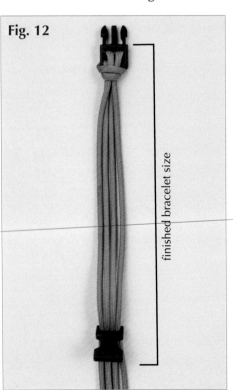

Fig. 12

finished bracelet size

STEP 5 To fuse the short cord ends to the short cords, fold each short cord end to the wrong side and leaving about 2" from buckle to ends, trim short cords. **Singe** (page 24), then quickly press the hot cord ends to the corresponding cords *(Fig. 13)*.

Tip: An alternative to fusing is to secure the ends to the cords with a narrow piece of tape (see page 10, *Fig. 14*).

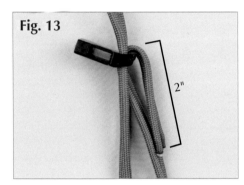

Fig. 13

2"

STEP 6 With the right side facing you, cross the working cords behind the standing cords *(Fig. 14)*.

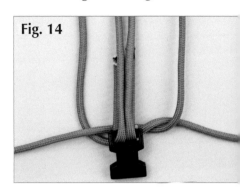

Fig. 14

STEP 7 Follow Steps 5-6, of **Loop And Knot Bracelet** (page 14) to tie a series of **Trilobite** knots until you reach the beginning buckle.

STEP 8 On the wrong side, thread the working cords under the last two knots (page 10, *Fig. 12*); **Trim and Singe** (page 24) the ends.

YOU CAN ALSO MAKE

For a 3½" long key fob, cut one 3' length of each cord color. For the standing cords, fold 12" of each cord over a metal split ring. Using the two longer cord ends as the working ends follow **Loop And Knot Bracelets**, page 14, Steps 2-9, to make your key fob.

Tip: Tape the ring and the top of the folded cords to your work surface.

SWITCHBACK BRACELETS

LOOP AND KNOT BRACELET
(shown on page 18)

STEP 1 Make a 4" long loop in one end of the cord. Make an 18" loop with the working end. Bring the working end over the left cord and tail and under the right cord, 2" below the top curve. *(Fig. 1)*.

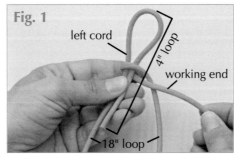

Fig. 1

left cord

4" loop

working end

18" loop

Tip: Taping the 4" loop cord end to the left cord will make it easier to hold all the cords as you begin knotting.

STEP 2 Wrap the working end over and under the right cord and over and under the left cord/tail *(Fig. 2)*.

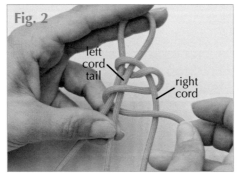

Fig. 2

left cord tail

right cord

STEP 3 Adjust and tighten the knots by pulling on the working cord *(Fig. 3)*. Gently slide the knots up the standing cords until the top loop is about 1" long. (Remove the tape, if used.)

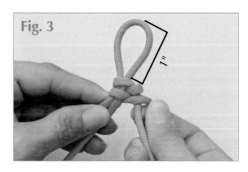

Fig. 3

1"

STEP 4 Tightening after each wrap *(Fig. 4)*, repeat Step 2 until the knotted section is 1" short of your finished bracelet size.

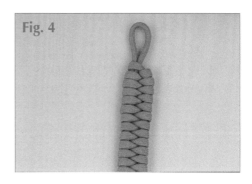

Fig. 4

Continued on page 18.

Switchback Bracelets continued.

STEP 5 Thread the working end under the last 2 knots *(Fig. 5)*; tighten. **Trim and Singe** (page 24) the end.

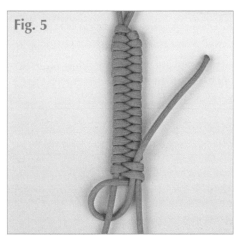

Fig. 5

STEP 6 Cut through the lower loop to make 2 equal length working cords. Use the working cords to make a **Diamond Knot** (page 23).

BUCKLE BRACELET

Tip: Taping down the top and bottom buckles may make it easier to tie knots around the standing cords.

STEP 1 Cut one 8' length of *each* paracord color.

STEP 2 Insert about 2" of each cord through one end of the buckle from front to back. Secure the cord ends to the corresponding cords with narrow pieces of tape *(Fig. 6)*.

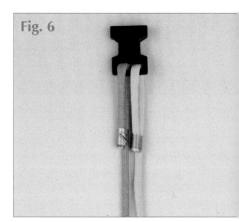

Fig. 6

*Tip: An alternative to taping is to fuse the ends to the corresponding cords. Refer to **Two Color Bracelet With A Buckle**, page 10, Step 2.*

STEP 3 Thread the cord ends through the remaining buckle piece and position the buckle at your finished bracelet size *(Fig. 7)*.

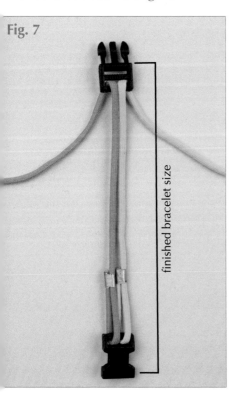

Fig. 7

finished bracelet size

STEP 4 Bring the left working cord over the left standing cord and under the right standing cord *(Fig. 8)*.

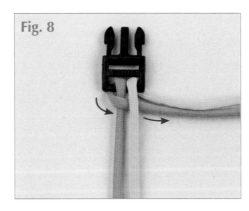

Fig. 8

STEP 5 Bring the right working cord over the right standing cord, under and around the left standing cord, and back under the right standing cord *(Fig. 9)*.

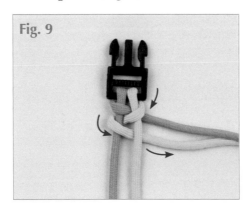

Fig. 9

STEP 6 Bring the right working cord over the right standing cord, under and around the left standing cord, and back under the right standing cord *(Fig. 10)*.

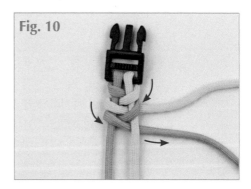

Fig. 10

STEP 7 Adjust and tighten the knots by pulling on the working cords and gently sliding the knots up the standing cords.

STEP 8 Alternating cord colors, repeat Steps 5-6 *(Fig. 11)* until you reach the beginning buckle.

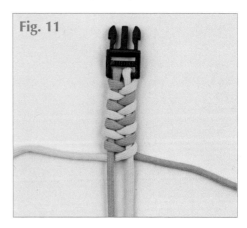

Fig. 11

STEP 9 Referring to page 18, *Fig. 5*, thread both working cord ends under the last knot made; tighten. **Trim and Singe** (page 24) the cord ends.

RIVER BAR BRACELETS

SHOPPING LIST

- [ ] 550 paracord (one 16' hank of **each** color)
- [ ] ⅝" wide side-release buckle (optional)
- [ ] utility scissors
- [ ] tape measure, ruler, or yardstick
- [ ] multi-purpose lighter

BUCKLE BRACELET

Note: Because all the cords are used equally there are no standing cords. The cords are called inner and outer depending on their position.

STEP 1 To attach the inner cords to the buckle, fold one cord in half and insert the loop through the lower opening of one buckle piece from back to front. Bring the cord ends through the loop *(Fig. 1)*; pull to tighten. Turn the buckle over.

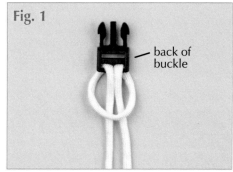

Fig. 1

back of buckle

STEP 2 To attach the outer cords, fold the second cord in half and insert the loop through the buckle top opening from back to front *(Fig. 2)*. Bring all four cords through the front loop *(Fig. 3)*.

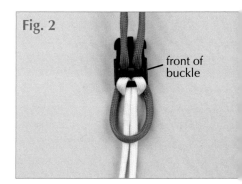

Fig. 2

front of buckle

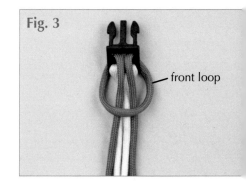

Fig. 3

front loop

STEP 3 Cross the outer cords behind the inner cords then bring the ends through the front loop; tighten *(Fig. 4)*.

STEP 4 Loop the inner cords over, then under the outer cords and, crossing behind the inner cords, bring the inner cord ends through the loops and over the outer cords *(Fig. 5)*.

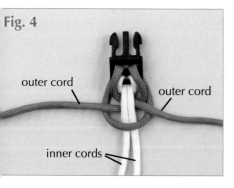

Fig. 4

outer cord

outer cord

inner cords

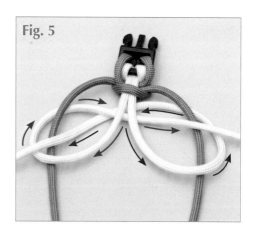

Fig. 5

Continued on page 22.

River Bar Bracelets continued.

STEP 5 Pull the working cords to tighten the knot *(Fig. 6)*.

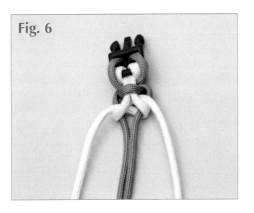

Fig. 6

STEP 6 Repeat Steps 4-5, to knot the inner cords around the outer cords *(Figs. 7-8)*, until you reach your finished bracelet size.

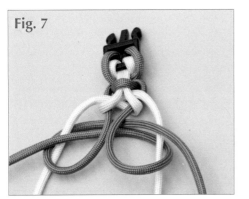

Fig. 7

Fig. 8

STEP 8 Working from front to back, insert all four cord ends through the remaining buckle piece. On the wrong side, thread the inner cord ends under the last knot made; **Trim and Singe** (page 24) the cord ends. Repeat to secure the outer cord ends under the next-to-last knot *(Fig. 9)*.

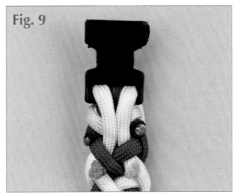

Fig. 9

LOOP AND KNOT BRACELET

Note: Because all the cords are used equally there are no standing cords. The cords are called inner and outer depending on their position.

STEP 1 Center one folded cord (inner) on the second cord (outer). Bring the left outer cord over the inner cords and behind the right outer cord. Bring the right outer cord behind the inner cords and through the loop created on the left *(Fig. 10)*.

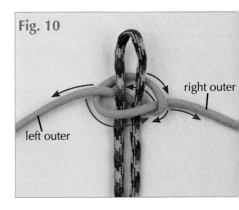

Fig. 10

right outer

left outer

STEP 2 Follow **Buckle Bracelet** (page 21, Steps 4-6), stopping when knotted section is 1" short of your finished bracelet size.

STEP 3 On the wrong side, thread the outer cords, only, under the last 2 knots; **Trim and Singe** (page 24) the ends *(Fig. 11)*.

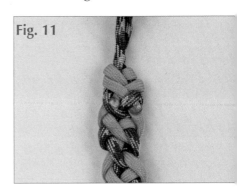

Fig. 11

STEP 4 Use the inner cords to make a **Diamond Knot** (page 23).

HOW TO TIE A DIAMOND KNOT

*A Diamond Knot makes a firm, round ball that is used
for all bracelets that close with a loop and knot.*

Note: *When tying a Diamond Knot, the right cord is always the right cord (shown in green) and the left cord is always the left cord (shown in red) even if they move to the opposite side of the knot. The numbers in () match the numbers on the Figs. where the cords go over or under each other. The placement for a Diamond Knot is approximately 1" from the end of your bracelet.*

STEP 1   Make a loop in the left cord. Bring the right cord behind the loop and over the left cord (*Fig. 1*).

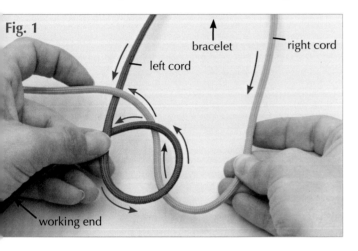

Fig. 1

STEP 2   Bring the right cord under the left cord working end (1), over the bottom of the loop of the left cord (2), and under the top of the loop of the right cord (3), forming a diamond in the center of the loops (*Fig. 2*).

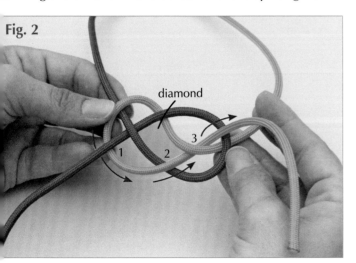

Fig. 2

STEP 3   Bring the left working end around the top of the knot (*Fig. 3*), under all the loops, and through the diamond from the back to the front. Bring the right working end around the bottom of the knot (*Fig. 4*), under all the loops, and through the diamond from the back to the front (*Fig. 5*).

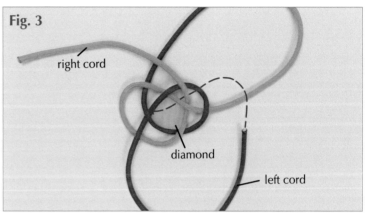

Fig. 3

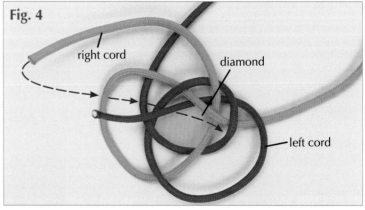

Fig. 4

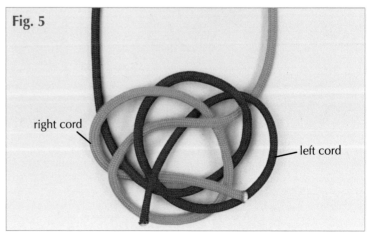

Fig. 5

Continued on page 24.

Diamond Knot continued.

STEP 4 Pull on all four cords until the loops tighten and start to form a ball. Pull and tug on the loops and cord ends until you are pleased with the shape of your knot *(Figs. 6-8)*.

Fig. 6

Fig. 7

STEP 5 Trim and Singe the ends *(Fig. 8)*.

Fig. 8

HOW TO TRIM AND SINGE

Caution: When working on these projects, always keep your fingers away from the flame and never touch a melted cord end until it has cooled completely. Adult supervision is required at all times.

Cord ends are singed (melted) with a lighter to keep them from fraying or to hold them in place. You should singe the ends when you cut a cord into lengths, anytime you finish using a cord and trim the ends, or as directed in your project instructions.

STEP 1 Trim paracord with sharp utility scissors. When you trim cords at the end of a bracelet, allow at least $1/8$ " of "melting room" *(Fig. 1)*.

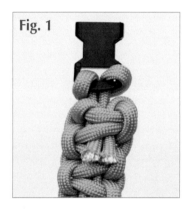
Fig. 1

STEP 2 Keeping your fingers safely away from the flame, give a quick (1 to 2 seconds) burst of heat to the cord ends *(Figs. 2-3)*.

Fig. 2

Fig. 3

Many thanks to Pepperell Crafts for providing the paracord used in these projects.

PEPPERELL CRAFTS
PEPPERELL BRAIDING COMPANY

Production Team: Designer – Patti Wallenfang; Design Assistant – Kelly Reider; Technical Writer – Jean Lewis; Technical Assistants – Lisa Lancaster and Mary Hutcheson; Editorial Writer – Susan Frantz Wiles; Senior Graphic Artist – Lora Puls; Graphic Artist – Becca Tally; Photo Stylist – Angela Alexander; Photographers – Jason Masters and Ken West.

Made in U.S.A.